To Jessica —
I miss you, come back near the lake!

Tiffany

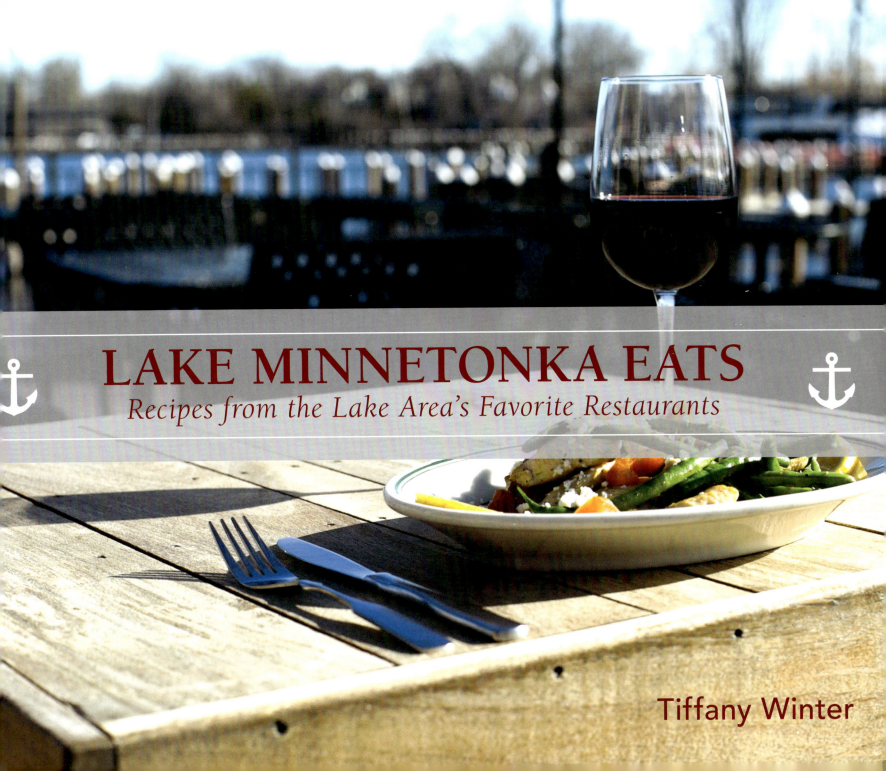

Cooks Bay Marketing
3343 Warner Lane
Mound, MN 55364

tiffany@cooksbaymarketing.com
www.lakeminnetonkaeats.com | www.cooksbaymarketing.com

LAKE MINNETONKA EATS

Copyright © 2015 by Cooks Bay Marketing.

All rights reserved. Except for short excerpts for review purposes, no part of this book may be reproduced or transmitted in any form by any means, electronic or mechanical, including photocopying, without permission in writing from the publisher.

Design by Jarvis Design
Edited by Mary Stacke

All photos submitted by restaurants and city chambers except the following:

Cover top right and bottom middle right, pages 3, 7, 9, 58, 62, 63, 65, 106, 128 by Al Whitaker

Cover bottom right, pages 1, 10, 11, 21, 22, 23, 25, 50, 51, 53, 54, 55, 57, 82, 85, 94, 95, 97, 122 by Michelle Patrice Photography

Cover bottom left and bottom middle left, pages 70, 71, 73, 98, 99, 101, 118, 121 by ESE Creative Solutions

Page 6 by Michael Cannon

Pages 13, 17 by MJFotography, Inc.

Page 75 (top), 77, 102, 103, 105 by A La Carte Creative Group

Page 93 by Ben Saltzman Photography

Printed in Minnesota by JS Print Group
First Edition, 2015

ISBN-13: 978-0-692-39197-6

10 9 8 7 6 5 4 3 2 1

To my parents, who made
Lake Minnetonka part of my life.

MENU

First Course – *A Taste of the Lake*
- Foreword by Stephanie March 5
- Introduction 6
- Lake Minnetonka Eats 8
- Farm-to-Table 12
- Lake Community Events 16

Main Course – *Recipes from the Lake Area's Favorite Restaurants*
- 318 Café 22
- 6Smith 26
- Al & Alma's Supper Club 30
- Bayside Grille 34
- Cast & Cru 38
- Coalition 42
- CōV Restaurant and Bar 46
- Dakota Junction 50
- Hazellewood Grill and Tap Room . . . 54
- Jake O'Connor's Pubic House 58
- Joey Nova's 62
- Lafayette Club 66
- Lago Tacos 70
- Lord Fletcher's 74
- Lunds & Byerlys Kitchen 78
- Maynard's 82
- Olive's Fresh Pizza Bar 86
- Patisserie Margo 90
- Scotty B's 94
- Sushi Fix 98
- The Narrows Saloon 102
- The Suburban 106
- Victor's on Water 110
- Wayzata Bar & Grill 114
- Wuollet Bakery 118

Dessert – *Beer Pairings*
- Excelsior Brewing Company 122
- Acknowledgements 126
- Index 127

FOREWORD

There's something about a lake town that just gets into a Minnesotan's heart. We dream about summers by a lake, afternoons spent playing on the water or parked on a park bench gazing out on the sun-dappled waves. We even love a winter lake, with our pop-up cities of ice fishing huts and shoveled rinks lit by parked cars. Lake life is the good life. And for so many, for so long, that lake of dreams has been Lake Minnetonka.

The history is well-known, that the city barons quickly found the boundless lake and set up summer homes as early as the 1850s. They knew a good hunk of water when they saw it.

But I grew up here in the boomtime of the 1980s when Lake Minnetonka and its surrounds had grown into, can you imagine, a suburb. It may have seemed less glamorous and winsome than in the days of the Big Island Amusement Park, at least to the city dwellers, but to us it was still a slice of heaven. While the inner ring claimed, as far as dining, that "there was no there, there" we had the only fine dining LeAnn Chin at Bonaventure Mall, right? Well, at the time that was cutting edge. Ask yourself: where would we be without cream cheese wontons?

We've had the Lafayette club, offering public picnics and a glimpse of the old grandeur. Lord Fletchers, which for generations has been a summertime haunt whether you're working the dock or just drinking on it. Al and Alma's has been cruising the lake since the 1980s, delivering a moveable feast unlike anything in the city.

But with time and tide, both the eating culture of the entire metro area and the dining landscape of cities and suburbs alike have evolved, changed, and become at once fascinating and of a national caliber. We have James Beard Award winners, the New York Times has visited. And so we find ourselves in the midst of a flourishing scene. Even out here, in lake town.

Anchored by homey and quaint Excelsior to the south, and glitzy well-heeled Wayzata to the north, the Lake Minnetonka eating scene is rich and varied. Take Dakota Junction out in Mound, using foods grown on nearby Gale Woods Farm to feed bikers on the Dakota Trail. Look at 6Smith bringing the best steak on the lake and a rooftop patio. CōV has changed the scene in Wayzata with fresh lake town design and easy eating all year round. Victor's on Water has one of those city chefs cooking regional Italian with local vegetables in ways you never knew were possible.

We've always known that lake life is the best life, and now we truly know how delicious it can be.

Stephanie March
Senior Editor, Food & Dining
Mpls. St. Paul Magazine

INTRODUCTION

Growing up on Cooks Bay, I developed a deep love for Lake Minnetonka. My childhood days were always filled with lake activities, and I still love living near the lake and being a part of our unique lake community. There's something magical about spending summer days sitting on the dock dipping your toes in the water or on the boat admiring the pinks and purples of the sunset. This love, combined with my foodie interests in cooking and restaurants, sparked my idea for the *Lake Minnetonka Eats* cookbook.

Lake Minnetonka has an amazing array of locally-owned restaurants, many new within the last year. I wanted to feature these unique businesses and the variety of food and drinks they serve. Each one has its place in the community, an interesting story and a local and loyal following. I truly enjoyed spending time in each restaurant learning their histories, meeting the chefs and owners and connecting with people that share the same passions.

Each week my mom and I try to make it to at least one farmers' market to see what's new and fresh. Oftentimes the ladies in my neighborhood go together to buy our produce and hit a restaurant for happy hour—it's one of my favorite things to do in the summer. Also, now that I've learned all that Gale Woods Farm has to offer, I know my nephews and I will frequent it often.

My whole life I have thoroughly enjoyed attending annual events held around the lake so I wanted to include the ones that have a strong food component. It's fun to celebrate with other lake lovers that share the same pride and local spirit of Lake Minnetonka.

It's an exciting time for restaurants—and diners—around Lake Minnetonka. I hope you relish learning about each place and trying out their delicious recipes as much as I did. Enjoy!

LAKE MINNETONKA EATS

THE LAKE LIFE

It's not just a destination; it's a way of life. Each community the lake touches embraces everything the lake offers with an abundance of boating and water activities, public parks lining the shore and summer festivals. Lake Minnetonka is even a hot spot in the cold winters with communities of ice houses popping up in each bay and winter sports competitions held on the ice. But all these recreational activities work up an appetite, and the lake area has a bounty of new and veteran dining establishments to satisfy every craving.

There's truly something for everyone—wood-fired pizza, Irish pub fare, classic American, mouthwatering prime steaks, amazingly fresh sushi. Getting to your dining destination is half the fun—by boat, car, bike, skis, snowmobile or whatever mode of transportation soaks up the best views of the lake.

TASTE OF THE LAKE

Whether it's a romantic dinner overlooking the lake, happy hour cocktails and appetizers on a sunny patio, a family breakfast or take-out to be enjoyed watching the sunset on the boat, each occasion is celebrated in the Lake Minnetonka neighborhood of restaurants.

Each restaurant has a story, a reason for putting out the food they do and being a part of the Lake Minnetonka community. There are the veteran restaurants that will always be a staple in the cuisine around the lake and many newcomers that are looking to shake things up. But one thing remains constant, their unwavering commitment to serving locals and visitors a taste of Lake Minnetonka.

FARM-TO-TABLE
LAKE AREA FARMERS' MARKETS

One of the best sources of locally-grown seasonal produce is the lake area farmers' open air markets. For years, it has been a great way to spend a morning or an afternoon by the lake, strolling around the market meeting local gardeners, bakers, butchers and more and picking fresh and flavorful produce, meats, herbs and flowers from the best the season has to offer. Held once per week from late spring through early fall in Excelsior, Mound and Wayzata, these popular destinations allow Lake Minnetonka community citizens to support local businesses.

The markets also connect local restaurants with farmers, and many have established relationships. 318 Café owner Matty O'Reilly met some of the local farmers at the Excelsior Farmers Market and started using their local produce in menu items. Beer bread made locally with Excelsior Brewing Company beer is often for sale as well as zucchini bread made from local zucchini.

Other homemade food products for sale—made locally, of course—include barbeque sauces, granola, "farm-to-bowl" dog food and treats, honey, chutneys and jams, gluten-free baking mixes, beef and turkey jerky, artisan whole-bean coffee and pure maple syrup. If looking at all the beautiful food makes your mouth water, a variety of local vendors and food trucks offer up such delicious items as refreshing fruit smoothies, French crêpes, sweet and savory strudels, fresh-squeezed lemonade and ethnic foods including samosas and curries. Local musicians strum their instruments and encourage market visitors to linger; it's the best way to do your weekly shopping.

GALE WOODS FARM

It doesn't get more local than this. Gale Woods Farm, located just west of Halsted Bay in Minnetrista, sells meat, produce and other goods grown or raised right on the farm. People from all over the Twin Cities visit the farm for unique educational (and just plain fun!) events like their Saturday Mornings on the Farm where all ages can explore the barn, meet animals and even assist a farmer with chores.

The park is the perfect place to spend the day outdoors. You can explore on your own, enjoy a true farm-to-table picnic by the lake or host your own event. It's a community gem that gives back by growing vegetables for the Mound Westonka Food Shelf and giving youth the opportunity to work in the gardens and learn about agriculture and leadership.

LAKE COMMUNITY EVENTS

The restaurants aren't the only draw for great grub around Lake Minnetonka. Each year the communities that surround the lake hold festivals and events that feature a variety of al fresco dining selections. It's not just your typical fair food as Lake Minnetonka eaters have an appetite for more eclectic food. Along with the corn dogs and cotton candy are slow-roasted meats, creative flatbread pizzas, zucchini and yucca fries, arepas filled with Latin concoctions of vegetables and meats and a whole lot of nosh served from spiffy trucks.

EXCELSIOR APPLE DAY

This special one-day event, held in September each year since 1929, celebrates apples and takes advantage of the peak apple season. Excelsior has a history with apples; the Excelsior Crab, a variety of crab apple, originated with resident and horticulturalist Peter Gideon. He also created the first apple to thrive in a Minnesota climate, the Wealthy Apple.

The celebration includes a baking contest of apple desserts, an apple pie eating contest, a beer and wine garden and a variety of local food vendors. People may come for the food but stay for the old-fashioned street dance, the street market of locally produced art, handicrafts and antiques, Happy Apple Kids' Corner and the Apple of the Lake 5K Race.

JAMES J. HILL DAYS

Held in Wayzata the weekend following Labor Day each year since 1975, James J. Hill Days is Wayzata's largest festival. It's a celebration centered around the lake with events for the entire family including a market on Lake Street, parade, water sports, live music, fireworks over Wayzata Bay and the always-popular Dachshund Races.

Local vendors and food trucks cook up everything from wood-fired pizza to street-style tacos to keep festival-goers fed and ready for more fun. 2014 marked the first ever Rails & Ales Craft Beer Festival with samples from over 20 breweries to wash it all down.

WAYZATA CHILLY OPEN

Being Minnesotans, winter doesn't get us down; in fact, it's embraced. Held on the ice of Wayzata Bay, the Chilly Open is a celebration of the season's elements. Every February since 1984, this unique frozen golf event draws crowds for some frozen fun.

But The 19th Hole tent is where the real action is, the Wayzata Chili Cook-off. Each year local restaurants bring their best chili in hopes of being named "the best" by celebrity judges. It's the best—and most delicious—way to warm up on a "chilly" day.

SPIRIT OF THE LAKES

This summertime festival held in Mound grows bigger and better each year. The weekend events are mainly lakeside at Surfside Park and include live stage performances, a wakesurf competition, boat rides that feature lake area history and a spectacular fireworks show.

The food court is also an attraction including enticing items such as rich homemade ice cream dipped to order, fish and chips, berry kabobs, state fair-style French fries and Wisconsin cheese curds. Down the road, the Gillespie Center hosts a bingo dinner. There's a tiki bar and beer tastings to top it all off.

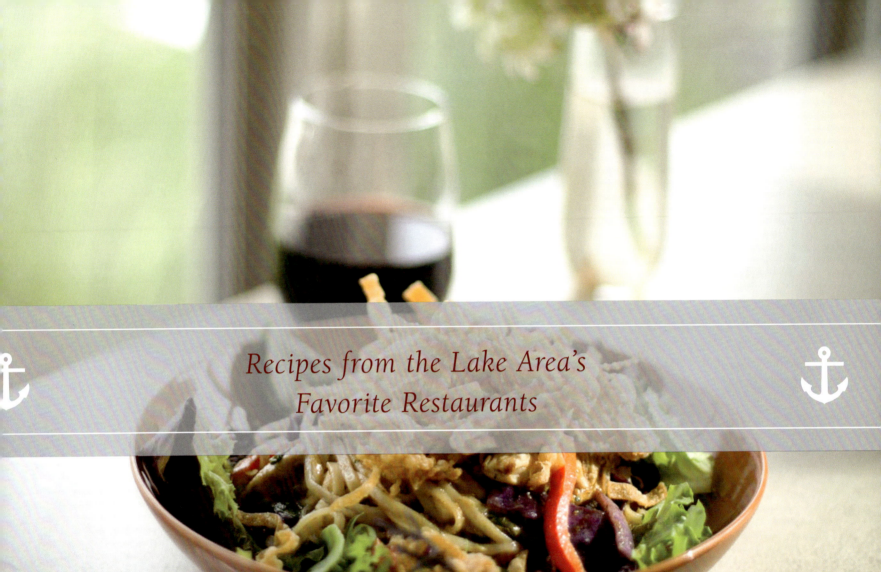

Recipes from the Lake Area's Favorite Restaurants

Founded in 2004 by cousins Matty O'Reilly and Tom Peterson, 318 Café is the lake area's premier café and coffeehouse by day, live music listening room by night. Located in the Excelsior Mill, 318 Café attracts loyal customers from all over the Twin Cities by hosting a variety of local and national musicians while serving food, coffee, craft beer and wine.

The music is obviously a big draw—the small stage has been graced with performances by Keri Noble, Martin Zellar, Michael Johnson and Adam Levy—but the scratch-made food is equally a star of the show. Tacos are a favorite as well as the homemade soups. The Southwest Quinoa Salad is a light and healthy option with a refreshing kick.

Whether it's to enjoy a latte next to the cozy fireplace in winter or a glass of wine and a cheese plate on the patio in summer, 318 Café is always a favorite.

 # 318 Café Southwest Quinoa Salad

INGREDIENTS

3 cups quinoa
½ cup tomato, chopped
¼ cup red pepper, chopped
¼ cup green pepper, chopped
1 jalapeno pepper, chopped
1 bunch scallions, minced
½ bunch cilantro, minced
½ red onion, minced

¼ cup olive oil
¼ cup fresh lime juice
1 tbsp. chili powder
½ tsp. cumin
½ tsp. cayenne pepper
Salt and pepper to taste

Tomatoes, sliced
Avocados, sliced
Corn chips

Rinse quinoa with cold water then cook in boiling, salted water for 10 - 12 minutes. Drain and chill.

Place tomatoes, peppers, scallions, cilantro and onion in a bowl with the quinoa. Whisk together olive oil, lime juice, chili powder, cumin, cayenne pepper and salt and pepper. Mix the salad ingredients with the dressing and serve with sliced tomatoes, avocado and corn chips. Serves 6 - 8.

NOTES

6SMITH

MEAT
FISH
DRINK

Opened in 2014, 6Smith is an answer for those seeking an authentic dining experience. This artisan-inspired restaurant with its industrial-chic vibe boasts expansive lakeside patios, private docks and Lake Minnetonka's only rooftop dining. The name, 6Smith, is derived from an 11th century term for blacksmiths and alludes to a passion for keeping authenticity, craftsmanship and artisanal technique at the forefront of everything it does. This philosophy is reflected in many handwrought details throughout the restaurant's design as well as the menu.

The restaurant features a large meat and seafood menu for eating, grazing or dining that is innovative, yet approachable. The focus is on high-quality food sourced from local purveyors, and craft cocktails, micro-brewed beers and wines from family-owned wineries.

A perfect example? The 6Smith Beef Cheek Nachos. This popular dish takes days, not minutes, to prepare. The beef is first cured overnight before being slow-roasted for hours. It's then paired with an authentic house-made poblano sauce and served with crispy tortilla chips. It's a crowd pleaser with rich depths of flavor.

6Smith Beef Cheek Nachos

INGREDIENTS

2 lbs. beef cheeks
2 tbsp. canola oil
1 clove garlic, minced
2 cups yellow onion, diced
1 ½ cups carrot, diced
1 ½ cups celery, diced
¼ cup tomato paste
⅔ cup red wine vinegar
3 cups beef stock
1 bay leaf
1 sprig each fresh thyme and rosemary

2 poblano peppers
1 jalapeno (optional)
2 tbsp. canola oil
1 cup lemon juice
½ tsp. salt and black pepper
2 tbsp. sour cream

Tortilla chips
Sharp cheddar cheese, shredded
Pickled red onions
Fresh cilantro

Place beef cheeks in a plastic bag with lots of salt and pepper; cure in the refrigerator overnight or for at least 2 hours. Brown the meat on all sides in oil using a heavy-bottom pot and being careful not to burn. Remove the cheeks from the pot and add the garlic, onion, carrots and celery; cook for 15 minutes. Add the tomato paste and cook for another 5 minutes. Deglaze with the red wine vinegar, then add the beef stock and herbs. Place the beef cheeks back into the pot, cover and bake at 350 degrees for 2 ½ hours.

To make the poblano sauce, coat the poblano peppers and jalapenos, if using, with the oil and roast them in the oven until skins are blistered and have brown patches. Take out of the oven and place the peppers in a bowl; cover with plastic wrap until they are easy enough to peel. Place the peppers in the blender and puree; add the remaining ingredients and blend until smooth.

To assemble, place a layer of tortilla chips on a plate. Evenly distribute beef and desired amount of cheese over the chips and broil until melted. Spread pickled onions on the top and drizzle with the poblano sauce. Garnish with fresh cilantro. Serves 3 - 4.

Located on Cooks Bay in Mound, Al & Alma's Supper Club was founded in 1956 by Al and Alma Quist. Now owned by Merritt and Daryl Geyen, it is Lake Minnetonka's longest operating restaurant. Open exclusively for dinner, today's modern restaurant embraces recipes that have spanned three generations.

The restaurant is open in all seasons, but summers are a great opportunity to take a boat cruise around the lake on one of Al & Alma's fleet. Breathtaking sights and sunsets, summer breezes and great food contribute to a perfect day or night out on the lake.

One menu item that is especially popular is the Camp Style Walleye. Coated in a cracker crumb mixture and cooked in a cast iron skillet, this is truly a favorite.

 # Al & Alma's Campstyle Walleye

INGREDIENTS

2 eggs

¼ cup milk

12 saltine crackers, crushed

Pinch of salt and pepper

Pinch of Old Bay seasoning

Pinch of parsley

3 tbsp. butter

2 (8 oz.) walleye filets

⅛ cup flour

Turn oven on to 350 degrees. Whisk eggs until well blended. Whisk in milk. Pour egg wash into a long shallow bowl. In a separate bowl mix crushed saltine crackers, salt, pepper, Old Bay seasoning, and parsley. Lightly dust the walleye filet in flour, shaking off excess. Soak both sides of the walleye in egg wash mixture. Coat walleye in cracker crumb mixture.

Melt butter in a cast iron skillet and add walleye; fry until one side is golden brown. Flip walleye and move cast iron pan into oven and bake for 10 minutes. Serve with lemons. Serves 2.

NOTES

Overlooking Excelsior Bay, Bayside Grille is one of the best places to watch the sunset, enjoy a meal and relax on the casual "Bohemian" deck setting. Locals like to grab a cocktail at the "Bottom's Up Boat Bar" built from a 20-foot C-Scow sailboat while listening to the live music for the evening.

Lake area history buffs know that the Bayside building itself was the former picnic pavilion for the Excelsior Amusement Park and more recently home to the legendary Mai Tai Restaurant's "Pu Pu Hut." In August 1999, Suite Life Catering purchased the Lake Minnetonka property including the BayView Event Center and Charter Cruises.

Bayside Grille's menu has something for everyone—and it's not your typical bar food. Customer favorites include the Bayside Minis, the Kabob Platter and their most popular appetizer, the Smoked Gouda and Lager Fondue. Flavored with lager beer and served in a crock with apples, sliced bread, vegetables and sliced, grilled chicken, it's great for sharing in any season.

 # Bayside Grille Smoked Gouda & Lager Fondue

INGREDIENTS

2 ½ tbsp. melted butter

2 ½ tbsp. yellow onion, diced

¼ cup all-purpose flour

⅔ cup beer

1 pinch ground mustard

1 ⅔ cups chicken stock

1 pinch ground nutmeg

7 oz. heavy cream

7 oz. smoked Gouda cheese, shredded

Kosher salt & ground black pepper to taste

Grilled rosemary-marinated chicken breast

Carrots & broccoli, blanched

Green apple, sliced

Breadsticks

Melt butter and sauté onion until soft. Add flour and cook for 5 minutes while stirring. Add beer, mustard, chicken stock, nutmeg and heavy cream; bring it to a boil for 10 min. Add cheese and stir. Add Kosher salt & ground black pepper to taste.

Serve fondue with rosemary marinated chicken breast, blanched carrots, broccoli, slices of green apple and breadsticks. Serves 4.

NOTES

CAST & CRU™
RESTAURANT

The Old Log Theatre in Greenwood has been an institution in the lake area for 75 years. In 2013, locals Greg and Marissa Frankenfield bought the Old Log to fulfill their dreams—his to own a theater and hers to open a restaurant. After a year of renovations to the entire building, the restaurant Cast & Cru opened in late summer of 2014. Cast & Cru is now drawing people from all over the Twin Cities to Greenwood—whether they have tickets to a show or not.

With a new state-of-the-art kitchen and the creative talent in the kitchen executing a modern American menu, the restaurant is as much of a draw as the theatre. Seasonal ingredients, many of which are grown in their on-site gardens on the property's 11 acres, are always a focus. The ingredients in the Horseradish-Crusted Salmon with Golden Beet Sauce are no exception.

Cast & Cru Horseradish-Crusted Salmon with Golden Beet Sauce

INGREDIENTS

Olive oil

4 (5-ounce) salmon steaks

½ fresh horseradish root, peeled and finely grated

3 large golden (yellow) beets

1 piece ginger root

3 garlic cloves

1 shallot, finely chopped

2 sprigs fresh thyme

2 cups fish stock

½ cup dry white wine

½ tbsp. balsamic vinegar

Salt and pepper to taste

1 tbsp. sour cream

Prepared cheese risotto

Preheat the oven to 400 degrees. Heat 2 tsp. olive oil in an ovenproof sauté pan and gently add the salmon steaks; sear for two minutes on each side. Remove and place steaks on a baking sheet; cover liberally with finely grated horseradish. Bake until golden brown (approximately 15 minutes).

Roast beets, ginger and garlic in a roasting pan with olive oil to coat for approximately one hour, then let cool and process in a juicer. (Alternatively, use a blender then place a fine mesh strainer over a large bowl and pour the liquid over; discard pulp.)

Sweat the shallot and thyme in a 12-inch skillet until shallots are translucent. Add fish stock and white wine, and reduce over low heat for 15 minutes. Add the golden beet juice, balsamic vinegar, salt and pepper. Stir until well blended and season with salt and pepper. Add sour cream, remove from heat and reserve.

To serve, form a small mound of cheese risotto in center of plate, and drizzle beet juice in a circle around it. Place salmon steak on top of risotto skin side up. Serves 4.

NOTES

coalition

2014 was a big year for Excelsior, and the opening of Coalition was a significant part of that. Set in a historic brick building right on Water Street, the restaurant is the creation of Chef Eli Wollenzien and reflects his passion for cooking with a diverse and inspired menu. Wollenzien and his partner and childhood friend, Deacon Eells, wanted their first solo venture to be in a close knit community, and our quaint city of Excelsior was the lucky winner.

"Coalition is about the combined efforts of chefs, cooks, servers, farmers, vineyards, and brewers and I see that partnership extending to our guests by providing the highest quality food and service in a warm and welcoming environment," Wollenzien says.

The quality and brightness of the food certainly stand out in his Strawberry Melon Salad. With grilled watermelon and fresh strawberries lightly dressed in a mint vinaigrette with accents of goat cheese and Marcona almonds—it's freshness on a plate.

 # Coalition Strawberry Watermelon Salad

INGREDIENTS

8 oz. mint leaves

½ cup sherry vinegar

Juice from 2 lemons

2 tbsp. honey

1 tsp. kosher salt

2 cups vegetable oil

1 lb. watermelon, peeled and prepared

4 oz. Bibb lettuce

4 fl. oz. mint vinaigrette

10 oz. strawberries, sliced

3 oz. goat cheese

15 - 20 Marcona almonds

2 tsp. coriander seeds, toasted

Place the first 5 ingredients in a blender. Pulse until mint is blended. With blender on low, drizzle in oil until fully incorporated.

Cut rind off of watermelon and cut watermelon in half. Slice 8 oz. rectangle pieces, about ½ inch thick from each half. Place one piece directly onto a very hot grill and warm for 30 - 60 seconds. Remove from grill and dice into ½" x ½" pieces. Dice the other piece of watermelon into ½" x ½" pieces.

In a mixing bowl, rip each Bibb lettuce leaf into 4 - 5 pieces. Toss Bibb lettuce with ½ of the mint vinaigrette and mound salad on large plate. Place all watermelon and strawberries in bowl and mix with remaining mint vinaigrette. Mound fruit on top of greens. Break up goat cheese into small chunks and place on top of salad. Place Marcona almonds around plate. Sprinkle top of salad with toasted coriander seeds. Serves 3 - 4.

NOTES

CōV
WAYZATA

CōV Restaurant and Bar is Lake Minnetonka's ticket to the east coast. Opened in 2014 by restaurateur Dean Vlahos, this upscale Wayzata restaurant lives and breathes the coastal life.

Take one step into the restaurant and you're instantly transported to Nantucket—it's the perfect escape from the cold Minnesota winters. But when boating season is upon us, the lakeside patio is a lovely setting for a meal with a view. The flawless service matches the quality of the food and atmosphere.

The food is what you'd find at a classy ocean-inspired spot with a seafood focus. CōV quickly became known for the crab cakes and oyster bar—one wall reads, "To eat an oyster is to kiss the sea on the lips," but the menu also includes other upscale offerings. If you want to stay in, CōV's Cioppino recipe is the perfect way to "get your coastal on" at home.

CōV Cioppino

INGREDIENTS

2 cups tomato juice

2 cups clam juice

2 tbsp. white vinegar

2 tsp. Tabasco sauce

1 tsp. Worcestershire sauce

1 tbsp. Old Bay Seasoning

¼ cup blended oil

2 tbsp. garlic, chopped

¼ cup shallots, chopped

½ cup white wine

12 oz. shrimp

8 oz. scallops

4 whole or 8 halved lobster tail

1 lb. mussels

1 lemon

Salt and pepper to taste

French baguette

Make the tomato fumet by mixing together first 6 ingredients; set aside.

Heat oil in a hot pan and sauté garlic and shallots until garlic is slightly brown. Deglaze the pan with the white wine. Add the seafood to the pan and cook for 30 seconds. Add the tomato fumet and cook until seafood is cooked. Add a squeeze of lemon and salt and pepper to taste.

Serve with a baguette. Serves 4.

NOTES

Dakota Junction is highly celebrated among bikers on the Dakota Rail Regional Trail—nearly 400,000 people use the trail each year—and those just looking for a fresh and healthy meal to take home to their family. Opened in Mound in 2013 by founder Stephanie Bolles, the compact restaurant's inspiration came from visits to nearby Gale Woods Farm which is located a mile further down the trail: "We fell in love with the farm and the beautiful bounty that came from it."

The freshness and quality of the food shine through at Bolles' farm-to-table restaurant. She works with local farms to source her eggs and meat and offers a chalkboard menu of seasonal items. Favorites include their homemade tots and bright-flavored soups, as well as a few chef-favorite Mexican dishes of huevos rancheros and carnitas.

The menu changes daily, but one constant is the ever-popular Thai Chicken Salad. Made from all organic ingredients and with the bell peppers and mixed greens sourced from Gale Woods Farm—this is a dish you can feel good about eating.

Dakota Junction Thai Chicken Salad

INGREDIENTS

8 oz. rice noodles

6 cups canola oil

½ of (12 oz.) package wonton skins

½ cup peanut butter

1 cup soy sauce

1 tsp. sesame oil

2 cloves garlic

1 tsp. sriracha or sambal (Asian chili paste) optional

½ cup fresh cilantro

½ cup + 1 tbsp. olive oil

1 red bell pepper

1 green bell pepper

1 yellow bell pepper

2 cups shredded red cabbage

2 cups chopped bok choy

12 oz. cooked chicken (preferably rotisserie chicken)

8 oz. mixed field greens or greens of your choice

½ cup unsalted peanuts, crushed

Using a stock pot bring 2 quarts of water to a boil. Add rice noodles and cook until they are soft but not mushy, about 2 - 3 minutes. Transfer noodles to ice water bath to stop cooking process.

Add canola oil to a stock pot and heat to 350 degrees. Cut wonton skins into thin ½" strips and fry in oil until golden. Place on paper towel to get rid of excess oil.

Prepare the sauce by blending peanut butter, soy sauce, sesame oil, garlic, sriracha or sambal (if using) and cilantro in a blender. While blender is running add ½ cup olive oil slowly until smooth and mixed well.

Core all peppers and cut into thin slices length wise. Shred cabbage into thin strips and cut bok choy into ½ inch pieces. Using a large skillet, add 1 tbsp. olive oil. Once skillet is hot add vegetable mix and cook until they start to soften. Add the cooked chicken and peanut sauce and toss until all coated. Add the cooked noodles and continue to cook until well blended and warm. Add water to thin out sauce if needed.

Place field greens in a salad bowl and add vegetable and noodle mix. Sprinkle crushed peanuts and wontons on center of mixture. Serves 4.

NOTES

Hazellewood
Grill and Tap Room

Hazellewood Grill and Tap Room in Tonka Bay, located at the site of the old Copperstein, has been a neighborhood gathering place for families and friends for over 10 years. Serving breakfast, lunch and dinner daily—as well as a popular happy hour and Sunday brunch—it's always a good time to visit "the Wood." Loyal patrons come year-round, sitting by the cozy fireplace in the winter and on the sunny patio in the summer.

It's no surprise that the restaurant has won several "Best Of" awards for best breakfast and best dinner when the food is consistently delicious. Executive Chef and Partner Scott Foster features a menu of classic comfort food where every member of the family can find something to enjoy. Menu favorites include the Meatloaf, the Pecan Walleye and the distinctive pastas. The Mediterranean Angel Hair pasta is particularly delicious with a light white wine sauce, sautéed vegetables and a salty punch of feta cheese.

Hazellewood Mediterranean Angel Hair Pasta

INGREDIENTS

12 oz. angel hair pasta

4 tbsp. olive oil

2 tbsp. shallots, julienned

⅔ cup spinach, wilted

⅓ cup canned roasted tomatoes, chopped

2 tbsp. jarred roasted red peppers, rinsed and sliced into strips

1 tbsp. Kalamata olives, pitted and sliced

¾ cup white wine

¼ cup garlic butter

1 tsp. each salt and pepper

2 tsp. fresh oregano, chopped

2 tbsp. feta cheese, crumbled

Garlic bread, toasted

Cook pasta according to directions on package. Heat olive oil in pan and sauté shallots until lightly brown. Add spinach, tomatoes, red peppers and olives. Add white wine and bring to a boil, scraping brown bits on the bottom of the pan, until reduced by half.

Add garlic butter, salt and pepper and stir until incorporated into the sauce. Add pasta to pan and toss well.

To plate, use tongs to mound up pasta as high as possible. Sprinkle with feta cheese and oregano. Serve with garlic bread. Serves 2.

NOTES

JAKE O'CONNOR'S
PUBLIC HOUSE

"Every small town in Ireland has a public house," says Dermot Cowley, a native of County Louth and owner of the Jake O'Connor's Public House. Excelsior got its very own public house in 2006 when Cowley replaced a former hardware store on Water Street with an ornate and lively pub and it was an instant hit winning numerous awards over the years.

The atmosphere is welcoming with the cozy booths, fireplace and dim lighting—the perfect escape from the winter cold. In the summer, the sidewalk tables are always packed. Grab a seat at the beautiful bar, built by Irish woodworkers, and relish one of the 16 beers on tap which include several Irish stouts and ales.

The Irish comfort food shares the menu with well-executed American steaks, salads and pastas. A cup of MacCafferty's Potato Soup is the best way to kick off an Irish meal followed by one of the "pub favorites" such as the creamy Chicken Pot Pie or Cork Corned Beef Sandwich. But if you can't go out, the Smoked Lamb Shank recipe is perfect for a St. Patrick's Day dinner at home.

Jake O'Connor's Smoked Lamb Shank

INGREDIENTS

4 lamb shanks

2 medium sweet yellow onions, peeled and halved

2 carrots, quartered

1 tbsp. whole black peppercorns

1 sprig fresh rosemary

2 quarts beef stock

1 lb. carrots, peeled

1 lb. parsnips, peeled

1 lb. sweet yellow onion, peeled and quartered

½ cup light brown sugar

⅓ cup Jameson Irish Whisky

1 tsp. kosher salt

½ tsp. ground black pepper

1 cup demi-glace

1 tbsp. fresh mint, diced

1 tbsp. whole grain mustard

Prepared mashed potatoes

Place lamb shanks in roasting pan and add onions, carrots, peppercorns, and rosemary. Add beef stock and cover tightly with aluminum foil. Cook in oven for 3 ½ hours at 350 degrees or until tender. When tender, take out of the oven and place lamb on a baking sheet; cool in refrigerator for one hour until firm. Once shanks are cooled smoke with cherry wood, either on range in perforated pan or in a gas smoker for 45 minutes with heavy smoke.

Remove the ends from the carrots and parsnips and cut in half lengthwise, then into approximately 1" wide half-moon shaped pieces. Boil the carrots and parsnips until tender, then drain. In a sauté pan, simmer carrot, parsnip, onion, brown sugar, whiskey, salt, and pepper on medium heat until sauce reduces by half.

In a small sauce pan, heat demi-glace, fresh mint and whole grain mustard until sauce becomes smooth and hot; do not boil.

To serve, place generous helpings of homemade mashed potatoes in the middle of the plates, lay the smoked lamb shank on the potatoes and top the shank with the candied root vegetables. Drizzle each dish with whole grain mustard and mint demi-glace. Serves 4.

Winner of numerous local awards for their New York-style pizza, Joey Nova's in Tonka Bay is obviously a local favorite. But chef and general manager Gary Ezell believes that it's more than a restaurant. "We have a unique opportunity to employ youth at an impressionable age so we focus on instilling morals and values and creating a team atmosphere." Ezell clearly has a distinctive passion about not only food, but life.

The pizzeria serves up a menu of traditional and specialty pizzas, pastas and grilled subs made from high-quality ingredients. Local ingredients are used whenever possible such as the spices and herbs from Windland Flats, a farm in Princeton, Minnesota. Even those with dietary restrictions can happily eat at Joey Nova's since they launched menu items with gluten-free-certified pizza crust and noodles. Ezell stresses that "We want everyone to enjoy coming here to eat."

The Baked Ziti has always been a hit. The pasta is accented by a sauce of Italian sausage, homemade marinara and fresh basil, then topped with three cheeses and baked to perfection. It's Italian comfort food at its best.

Joey Nova's Baked Ziti

INGREDIENTS

4 cups penne noodles

2 cups marinara sauce

6 oz. Italian sausage, cooked and crumbled

½ cup ricotta cheese

1 cup mozzarella cheese, shredded

2 tbsp. parmesan cheese, shaved

2 tbsp. Italian-style bread crumbs

Garlic bread, toasted

Preheat oven to 450 degrees. Boil penne pasta according to package instructions or until al dente. Meanwhile, heat a large oven-proof sauté pan over medium heat and add marinara sauce. Add the crumbled, browned sausage and heat through. Add the drained pasta to the pan and toss well to coat all of the noodles evenly.

Break the ricotta cheese into small pieces and place evenly over the pasta. Spread the mozzarella evenly over all and sprinkle the parmesan on top. Top with the bread crumbs and place in the oven for 3 - 5 minutes until mozzarella is evenly melted and starting to brown.

Using a rubber spatula, slide the pasta evenly into pasta bowls. Serve with garlic bread. Serves 2.

NOTES

Lafayette Club's history goes back to the original hotel which opened on July 4, 1882 and was built by railroad magnate James J. Hill. Billed as "the finest hotel west of New York City," its guests included General Ulysses S. Grant, Vice President Adlai Stevenson, President Chester Arthur, President William Howard Taft and many governors of the State of Minnesota. The current clubhouse was built in 1925 on Crystal Bay and through the years has evolved from a stately hotel to a beautiful gathering place for families and friends to enjoy.

The club has both formal and casual dining options but both share the same menu of American classics with modern twists. Executive Chef Jake and his staff work hard to keep things fresh and interesting. With all-you-can-eat crab nights, the famous prime rib buffets and family bingo nights with a buffet that all ages can enjoy, there's always something for members to look forward to in the dining room.

The Cauliflower-Pancetta Soup is a great platform for adding different proteins: Hawley recommends trying smoked chicken or salmon, blackened shrimp or duck confit. The recipe, as with many of the club's featured dishes, is a collaboration of ideas from the entire team in the kitchen. Chef Jake stresses that he has a seasoned crew of hard-working people who have a common love for good food—this soup is certainly a reflection of that.

Lafayette Club Cauliflower-Pancetta Soup

INGREDIENTS

5 lbs. cauliflower florets, divided

2 tbsp. olive oil

½ tsp. sea salt

½ tsp. ground pepper (black or white)

½ tsp. chili flakes

8 oz. pancetta or bacon, diced medium

1 cup celery, diced small

1 cup yellow onion, diced small

¼ tsp. nutmeg

6 cups chicken broth

4 cups half & half

Sunflower seeds, toasted

Preheat oven to 400 degrees. Toss 1 lb. of the cauliflower florets in the olive oil, sea salt, pepper and chili flakes and spread evenly on a baking sheet. Roast in the oven until tender or slightly browned around the edges; let cool. Steam the remaining cauliflower florets in a pot on the stove until soft; set aside.

In a two-gallon pot, render the pancetta over medium-low heat until moderately crispy. Remove from pot with a slotted spoon and reserve for later. Sauté the celery and onions together, covered, in the excess pancetta fat (or 2 tbsp. olive oil) and nutmeg until soft. Add the chicken broth and bring to a simmer. Once hot, add the half and half and the steamed florets. Once mixture is hot, transfer in batches to a blender and blend until smooth and silky. Return the pureed mix to the pot and mix in the roasted florets and the rendered pancetta.

Serve in bowls and season as desired—try starting with a tsp. of salt, ½ tsp. of pepper, a dash of sherry vinegar and a splash of Tabasco, mixed together or simply a drizzle of good quality extra virgin olive oil. Garnish with toasted sunflower seeds for crunch. Serves 10 - 12.

NOTES

Popular Excelsior taco spot Lago Tacos has been serving up "unauthentic authentic" Mexican food since 2013. Owner Roger Burks was boating with his wife and friends when they realized the lake area needed an "upscale taco joint." After 30 years in the restaurant business, this was the first restaurant he started on his own and has since expanded to a second location in Uptown with plans for future locations.

The menu features classic items such as tacos you'd find on the streets of Mexico, innovative dishes with "Fun Mex" flavors and over 20 different tequilas. The breakfast at Lago Tacos is not to be missed—creative interpretations of traditional Mexican breakfast items hale from the dishes Burks makes for his kids on Christmas morning.

Tacos Al Pastor are made with pork marinated "in the style of the shepherd" and are the result of recipe experimentations of Burks and his kitchen crew from Mexico. The staff at Lago Tacos is more like a big family: "We found some great employees and their family members now work for us too."

 # Lago Tacos Tacos Al Pastor

INGREDIENTS

2 dried guajillo chili peppers

¼ cup + 2 tbsp. hot water

6 slices red onion, ½ inch thick

2 tbsp. orange juice

¼ cup sauce from canned chipotle peppers

2 tsp. fresh garlic, chopped

Pinch ground white pepper

3 tbsp. white vinegar

Pinch ground cinnamon

1 ½ tsp. salt

1 ½ lbs. pork tenderloin, sliced ⅓ inch thick

3 slices fresh pineapple, peeled or canned pineapple

8 - 12 corn or flour tortillas

1 ½ cups salsa, preferably green salsa

1 avocado, peeled and sliced (optional)

½ cup queso fresco (optional)

To first make the marinade for the pork, preheat oven to 350 degrees. Remove stems and seeds from guajillo peppers and roast in oven until they turn a very dark color. Remove and rehydrate in the hot tap water for 5 - 10 minutes. Place the onion slices on a hot grill to achieve grill marks. Then place 3 of the slices into a blender along with the next ingredients through the salt including the peppers and the water used to rehydrate, and puree until smooth. Marinade should be a medium-thick consistency. Marinate sliced pork loin with the Al Pastor marinade for 12 - 24 hours.

Preheat grill to medium heat and place pineapple on grill. Grill both sides to achieve nice char marks then pull off grill to cool. Once slightly cooled, dice the remaining grilled onion slices and pineapple and mix together. Grill pork until desired doneness and dice into ½ inch cubes. Place tortillas on grill to warm up then fill each with 2 - 3 ounces pork. Top with pineapple and red onion, salsa and avocado slice and crumble queso fresco over top. Serves 4.

NOTES

Lord Fletcher's has truly been an institution in the Twin Cities dining and bar scene since its establishment in 1968. An all-season hot spot, there is always something happening at "Fletcher's." In the summer, the sunny days pack the enormous open deck with people coming by land or sea, volleyball games are in play on the sand courts and live music keeps the atmosphere hopping. The winter hosts broomball games on the ice, cozy dining by the fireplace in the rustic Main Dining Room and a sports bar atmosphere to catch your favorite game in The Oar House.

For those looking for fine dining, the Main Dining Room is where you'll find inventive steak and seafood specialties and gourmet burgers and sandwiches. Lead by Executive Chef Thomas Pivec, the kitchen puts out consistently remarkable meals, and an in-house sommelier allows for an impressive selection of wines to pair with each dish. Lord Fletcher's continues to earn accolades for its food, atmosphere and service.

The "Shoreline Specialties" are seafood favorites and the Roasted Scottish Salmon Harvest Grain Salad lives up to the name. Scottish salmon, dressed with fresh herbs, sits on a bed of vegetables and quinoa. It's an elegant meal perfect for lakeside dining.

Lord Fletcher's Roasted Scottish Salmon Harvest Grain Salad

INGREDIENTS

4 tablespoons oil, divided

1 ⅓ cups celery, chopped

1 ⅓ cups carrots, chopped

1 ⅓ cups onion, chopped

2 tbsp. garlic, chopped

2 tbsp. shallots, chopped

4 cups red quinoa

8 cups chicken stock

Salt and pepper to taste

4 oz. bacon, diced large

2 cups kale, julienned

4 (6 oz.) Scottish or Norwegian salmon fillets, skin on

Fresh herbs to taste

Preheat oven to 350 degrees. Sweat the celery, carrot and onion in 2 tbsp. of the oil in a pot. Add garlic and shallots and cook until aromatic. Add the quinoa and chicken stock, cover and simmer over low heat until the stock is absorbed and the quinoa is tender, about 17 minutes. Uncover, fluff with a fork and let cool. Season with salt and pepper.

Crisp bacon in a sauté pan. Add kale and sauté until tender. In another pan, heat the remaining oil in an ovenproof skillet over medium-high heat. Season salmon pieces with salt and pepper. Place salmon in skillet skin side down. Cook for 2 minutes on each side. Place skillet in oven and roast for an additional 7 - 10 minutes until medium.

Divide quinoa mixture among plates. Top with salmon skin side up and fresh herbs. Serves 4.

NOTES

LUNDS & BYERLYS KITCHEN
SHOP • EAT • DRINK • EXPLORE

In 2014, Wayzata got a first-of-its kind food destination in the Twin Cities featuring prepared food offerings, a wine and beer bar, a tailored selection of groceries and more—all in one space. Lunds and Byerlys Kitchen is the perfect spot to pick up dinner and still put a great-tasting meal with high-quality ingredients on the table. It's truly a sight with options of made-to-order sandwiches, sushi, a salad and hot food bar, cut-to-order meats and more.

Equally as much of a draw is the dine-in area and full display kitchen where patrons can watch their food being made after ordering from a server or an iPad. The wine and beer bar features an impressive selection of hyper-local craft beers on tap and wines from around the world. Chef Gabe Stockinger focuses on creative and quality dishes with food selections including burgers, stone-oven pizzas, seasonal entrées and weekly meat and seafood flights. A customer favorite is the Pub Burger with its accents of bacon beer jam and mustard aioli. Both condiment recipes make extra, and the aioli is so good it can be used on anything or even as a marinade.

 # Lunds & Byerlys Kitchen Pub Burger

INGREDIENTS

1 lb. applewood smoked Lunds & Byerly's Bacon, diced small
2 ½ lb. yellow onion, diced
1 cup balsamic vinegar
1 ½ cups red wine vinegar
1 cup sugar
1 cup light brown sugar
¾ bottle beer
1 tbsp. liquid smoke

1 ½ cups whole grain mustard
1 cup heavy mayo
¾ cup sour cream
⅓ cup yellow mustard
1 clove garlic, finely minced
1 tbsp. cider vinegar

2 traditional buns, egg style
2 (⅓ lb.) grass-fed beef patties
4 oz. smoked Gouda cheese, sliced
¼ cup bacon beer jam
¼ cup mustard aioli

To make the bacon beer jam, cook bacon in a low wide cooking pot, like a braiser. Remove bacon from pan and most of the fat. Sauté onions in remaining bacon fat, then add the remaining ingredients through the liquid smoke and cook down to a jammy sauce. Cool and refrigerate until needed.

Make the mustard aioli by mixing the mustard through the vinegar ingredients by hand.

Lightly butter the inside of the buns and place on a hot grill to toast. Grill burgers to desired temperature, top with smoked Gouda and bacon beer jam and cook until cheese is melted. Serve with a side of mustard aioli. Serves 2 with additional bacon beer jam and mustard aioli.

NOTES

Maynards

Maynard's has been a favorite spot of locals—and the entire metro area—to dine and drink on the lake since it was established in 1998. Located on the historic land that was formerly occupied by the Excelsior Amusement Park, the restaurant is known for its sweeping views of Excelsior Bay. Locally owned and operated by the Stevens family, Maynard's takes pride in giving back to the community with fundraisers consistently on the calendar.

The American casual menu satisfies a variety of tastes with a large selection of appetizers, burgers, pastas and reasonably priced steak and seafood entrees. People may first come to Maynard's for the view but keep coming back for the food—giant onion rings, the famous Frannie's Chicken Salad and the abundant Sunday brunch buffet are just a few of the favorites.

Maynard's is also a destination for those with special dietary needs due to the selection of low carb and low fat items and an entire gluten-free menu. No one would guess from the taste that the Skinny Chicken is a light and gluten-free entrée. Chicken sautéed with green beans and Roma tomatoes then dressed with avocado and feta is sure to please no matter what your diet.

 # Maynard's Skinny Chicken

INGREDIENTS

3 oz. green beans

1 lemon

 2 tbsp. olive oil

1 (7 oz.) chicken breast

1 Roma tomato

1 avocado

Pinch of salt and pepper

1 tbsp. feta cheese

Cook green beans in salted, boiling water for two minutes; immediately place in a bowl of ice water to prevent further cooking. Cut two slices of lemon and reserve for garnish.

Heat olive oil in a non-stick sauté pan. Cut chicken into 1 inch strips and add to pan. While chicken is cooking dice the tomato and avocado. Once chicken is nearly done, take the rest of the lemon and squeeze juice on to chicken. Add tomato, avocado, green beans and a pinch of salt and pepper and warm through. Top with feta cheese and lemon slices. Serves 1.

NOTES

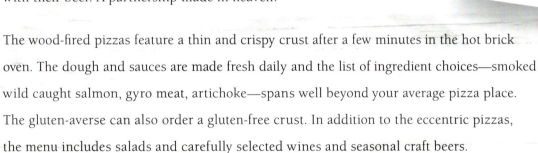

Excelsior got its own Neapolitan-style pizzeria when owners Jason Bailey, John Marshall and Duff Smith opened Olive's Fresh Pizza Bar on Water Street in 2015. Currently there are two locations of this local pizzeria with the first in White Bear Lake. Olive's Fresh Pizza Bar offers up pizza at the Excelsior Brewing Company on select evenings for those looking for some nibbles with their beer. A partnership made in heaven?

The wood-fired pizzas feature a thin and crispy crust after a few minutes in the hot brick oven. The dough and sauces are made fresh daily and the list of ingredient choices—smoked wild caught salmon, gyro meat, artichoke—spans well beyond your average pizza place. The gluten-averse can also order a gluten-free crust. In addition to the eccentric pizzas, the menu includes salads and carefully selected wines and seasonal craft beers.

The Fresno Pizza already has a strong following. The gourmet ingredients of caramelized fig, smoked pancetta, fresh sliced pear and a variety of cheeses lay on top of a light garlic-infused olive oil base. The standout is the aged balsamic cream which makes the pizza shine. Serve this pizza when you're trying to make an impression.

 # Olive's Fresh Pizza Bar Fresno Pizza

INGREDIENTS

4 fresh figs, halved lengthwise

2 tbsp. melted butter

2 tbsp. brown sugar

1 garlic clove, minced

⅓ cup extra-virgin olive oil

1 cup mozzarella cheese, shredded

1 lb. prepared pizza dough

½ red onion, thinly sliced

⅓ cup gorgonzola cheese, crumbled

1 ½ oz. smoked pancetta, chopped

Gourmet greens

Aged balsamic cream, to taste

1 pear, sliced

Parmesan cheese, shaved

Preheat broiler. Arrange figs, cut sides up, on a large shallow baking pan. Sprinkle sugar evenly over fruit and broil 2 to 3 inches from heat until most of sugar is melted and deep golden in places, 3 to 5 minutes.

Place a pizza stone on the bottom rack of a cold oven and set the oven to 475 degrees. Stir together garlic and oil. Stretch dough into a thin disc and brush with the garlic oil. Sprinkle the mozzarella cheese evenly over the dough and top with the caramelized figs, red onion, gorgonzola and smoked pancetta.

Slide the pizza onto the hot stone and bake for 7 minutes, or until bubbly and golden brown. Top with the gourmet greens, aged balsamic cream, fresh sliced pear and shaved parmesan. Makes 1 pizza.

NOTES

PATISSERIE Margo

Owned by Eric and Margo Bredeson, Patisserie Margo is a family business that stemmed from Margo's experience as a Pastry Chef. Not only is it family-owned, they treat their customers like family; it's been referred to as the "bakery version of 'Cheers'" where everybody knows your name. Located right in downtown Excelsior, it's the perfect place to grab your favorite pastry and a warm cup of coffee before a leisurely stroll down Water Street or a baguette on your way home for the day.

Everything in the bakery is made from scratch with no preservatives or trans fats, and the decadent flavors confirm the quality of the ingredients. Sinful cookies, buttery croissants and the black bottom cupcakes are a few of the favorites. The French sweets are tantalizing, but the savory side of the menu with quiche, sandwiches, soups and bread is just as much a draw.

The Linzer Torte is particularly delightful due to the freshly grated lemon zest, and the flavors are even better after a day or two. If you're looking for a beautiful dessert that's sure to impress, this is it.

 # Patisserie Margo Linzer Torte

INGREDIENTS

2 cups flour, sifted

½ lb. almonds, ground

1 cup granulated sugar

¼ tsp. ground cloves

2 tsp. ground cinnamon

1 tbsp. cocoa powder

2 sticks of butter, softened

2 egg yolks

2 tsp. kirsch or rum

½ tsp. lemon zest, grated

⅔ cup raspberry jam

1 egg, beaten

Place all dry ingredients in a mixing bowl. Mix with paddle; then add butter, egg yolks, liquor and lemon zest. Mix on low speed just until ingredients come together.

Knead dough only enough to create a ball of dough. Wrap in plastic wrap and flatten into a disc. Let stand for one hour.

Roll out ⅔ of the dough to line a 10" cake or tart pan. Spread with the raspberry jam. Roll out remaining ⅓ dough, cut into strips and decorate the top of the tart in a lattice pattern. Brush the rim of the pastry and the lattice with the beaten egg, being careful not to get egg into the jam. Bake in a preheated 350 degree oven for 35 minutes, or until pastry is golden brown. Serve warm or cold.

NOTES

Scotty B's
RESTAURANT

In February of 2015, Scotty B's Restaurant celebrated its 25th anniversary. Known as one of the most family-friendly spot in Mound, the restaurant is also deeply engrained in the community. Owners Scott Bjorlin and Scott Price make it a point to give back to the people in the city and organizations that support them through sponsorships and donations to area sports teams, the local schools and community events.

Families and friends come for the American food and the comfortable atmosphere; it's a social place from breakfast through dinner where Bjorlin spends much of his time floating from table to table catching up with customers. Many of the menu items are made from scratch and the food is always consistently satisfying.

Customers love Scotty's Favorite Breakfast, the made-in-house burgers and the homemade soups with warm breadsticks. The creamy German Sauerkraut soup is especially popular—with potatoes, polish sausage and lots of sauerkraut, it's hearty enough for a meal.

Scotty B's German Sauerkraut Soup

INGREDIENTS

1 gallon water

8 cups dehydrated potatoes

2 ½ lb. cooked polish sausage, diced

3 lb. sauerkraut

¼ cup Lawry's seasoned salt

½ cup chicken base paste

6 cups canned diced tomatoes

4 cups heavy whipping cream

Place all ingredients except cream in a pot and simmer until the potatoes are soft. Add cream and warm through. Serves 8 - 10.

NOTES

In 2012, Sushi Fix started its journey as a new business—literally a journey, as it was a food truck. Owner and Chef Enkhbileg "Billy" Tserenbat, then an Executive Chef at another sushi restaurant, noticed the food truck trend taking off and jumped at the chance to go out on his own. But it wasn't without skepticism; sushi from a truck may not initially sound appetizing, but the high-quality rolls and the undoubtedly fresh ingredients made it a fast success as the first sushi food truck in the Midwest.

Later that summer when the Sushi Fix truck was a food vendor at James J. Hill Days, a customer suggested to Billy that he open a brick and mortar location in Wayzata. "It was the perfect idea with easy access to Lake Minnetonka and a short trip from Minneapolis." One month later the lease was signed.

The restaurant features a unique and extensive menu of sushi and Japanese favorites, but the Japanese whisky bar and vast sake selection are just as much a draw—ask about the "secret sake menu" and you'll be pleasantly surprised. Dedicated to featuring seasonal, fresh ingredients, Sushi Fix has fresh fish delivered six days a week. The Wayzata Trojan Roll is a colorful and delicious menu standout.

 # Sushi Fix Wayzata Trojan Roll

INGREDIENTS

Soy paper

⅔ cup cooked sushi rice

2 oz. tuna, thinly sliced

2 oz. salmon, thinly sliced

2 oz. walu (butterfish), thinly sliced

2 oz. red snapper, thinly sliced

½ cucumber, sliced into thin strips

½ avocado, peeled, pitted and sliced

¼ cup fresh cilantro, chopped

Chili oil

Ponzu sauce

Creamy wasabi sauce

Place soy paper on a sushi mat (maki su). Use your hands to spread a thin layer of rice to cover the soy paper, leaving one inch from top edge uncovered. This will help the roll to stick together.

Arrange the fish across the center of the rice first, then place the cucumber, avocado and cilantro on top. Hold the fillings in place with your fingers and begin rolling the edge of the sushi mat that is closest to you. Keep rolling while pressing down to keep the roll tight and firm to make a complete roll.

Use a very sharp knife and cut the roll into 10 pieces. To serve, place cut side up and drizzle with a little chili oil, ponzu sauce and creamy wasabi sauce. Makes 1 roll.

NOTES

The Narrows Saloon in Navarre, so named for the Narrows channel of Lake Minnetonka about a mile away, is the go-to spot to hear live music and get your boogie on. Owner Jim Anderst has made a name for the bar and restaurant in the Twin Cities with a jam-packed entertainment calendar of blues, classic rock, R&B, dance and country bands almost every night of the week. The lively tavern draws everyone from bikers in their leathers to boaters in Dockers with reasonable prices, a selection of the area's finest craft beers and great grub.

The food is as much of a draw as the music at this local watering hole. The menu boasts spicy Cajun dishes like the Blackened Salmon and Blackened Fish Wrap for those who like zip; for those who prefer a mild taste, favorites include the homemade Dirty Pork Stew and the wide selection of burgers. The weekend breakfast is also a hit with a Lobster Bennie that you'll want to write home about.

The Shady Island Chicken Sandwich is the new employee favorite; a buttermilk-dipped, lightly fried chicken breast is kicked up a notch with sweet pickle spicy slaw and sriracha garlic mayo. It's a zippy accompaniment to the live blues band on stage.

 # The Narrows Saloon Shady Island Chicken Sandwich

INGREDIENTS

2 garlic cloves, finely grated

½ cup mayonnaise

1 tbsp. Louisiana-style hot pepper sauce

½ small red onion, thinly sliced

1 jalapeno, thinly sliced

4 cups cabbage, thinly sliced

½ cup bread and butter pickle slices

¼ cup pickle juice

Vegetable oil for frying

2 cups all-purpose flour

1 tbsp. ground black pepper

½ tsp. kosher salt, plus more for seasoning

1 cup buttermilk

2 (8 oz.) skinless, boneless chicken breasts, halved crosswise

4 fresh Brioche bakery buns

2 tbsp. unsalted butter, room temperature

Make the spicy mayo by mixing garlic, mayonnaise and hot pepper sauce in a small bowl; cover and chill. To make the slaw, mix onion, jalapeno, cabbage, pickles and pickle juice in a large bowl; cover and chill.

Warm oil in a deep skillet. Whisk flour, pepper and ½ teaspoon salt in a shallow bowl. Pour buttermilk into another bowl. One piece at a time, dredge chicken in flour mixture, shaking off excess; dip in buttermilk, allowing excess to drip. Coat again in flour mixture and shake off excess. Fry the chicken breasts in the hot skillet until golden brown and a thermometer registers 350 degrees, about three minutes per side. Transfer to a wire rack or paper towel and season with salt.

Spread cut side of buns with butter and cook in skillet until crisp, about one minute. Spread both sides with spicy mayo, add chicken breasts and top with the cabbage slaw. Serves 4.

NOTES

The Suburban
Burgers • Pizza • Beer

The Suburban has been "putting the urban in suburban" since 2014 when owners Cindy, Kelsey and Ashley Berset saw the need for a sports bar in Excelsior. Lifelong residents, the mother and daughters team wanted to realize their dream of opening a sports bar and restaurant in the city they love. With an abundance of TVs and the kitchen turning out burgers and pizza, they've done just that.

The Suburban has a social atmosphere where locals go to catch the game while having a few beers and families celebrate the little league win over pizza. The menu features creative burgers—the Meat Your Maker with bacon, a hot dog and assorted fixings being a favorite—a variety of pizzas and your favorite sports bar appetizers. Local vendors are used whenever possible for food ingredients, and several of the beers are from breweries in the western suburbs.

The Burb Sauce is a condiment bursting with flavor that spices up any burger or sandwich. It is also delicious as a dip with fries or tator tots.

The Surburban Burb Sauce

INGREDIENTS

4 cups good mayonnaise

½ cup ketchup

2 ½ tsp. sriracha

½ cup sweet pickle relish

2 ½ tsp. kosher salt

½ tsp. black pepper

1 tsp. fresh lemon juice

1 tsp. onion powder

2 tbsp. sport peppers, diced

Mix all ingredients together and refrigerate to let flavors meld. Store up to 1 week.

Serve on burgers and sandwiches or as a dip with fries and tater tots.

NOTES

Located on a prime corner of Water Street, Victor's On Water has quickly become a hot spot in downtown Excelsior. Opened during the 2014 restaurant boom in Excelsior, owners Eric Paulson and Janel Olson (both natives to Excelsior) and Executive Chef Phillip Becht created a niche by crafting upscale Italian cuisine made with high-quality seasonal ingredients, many of which are sourced locally and from the upper Midwest.

Large windows line the fine dining restaurant, enticing those walking by to stop in. Inside, the sleek space is accented by exposed bricks and a glow from the bar and open kitchen. The menu features pasta made in-house daily, inviting vegetable sides and remarkable large plates. General Manager and sommelier Matt Bolles created a noteworthy wine and beverage program to compliment any and all dishes.

The Neopolitan-style pizza is a canvas for the team to experiment with different ingredients, "We have a lot of fun coming up with combinations and names for our pizzas." Although the pizzas served at the restaurant may seem flawless, a pizza made at home can be "perfectly imperfect and delicious." The dough recipe allows people to create their own pizza masterpiece and comes with advice from the chef: if possible, use the weight measurements of ingredients versus volume because they are more accurate, and keep toppings to a minimum so the crust maintains a balance of crunch and chew.

Victor's on Water Pizza Dough

INGREDIENTS

5.5 oz. (1 cup + 1 tbsp.) Italian "00" flour

5.5 oz. (1 cup + 1 tbsp.) all-purpose flour

⅓ oz. (1 tsp.) fine sea salt

¼ oz. (¾ tsp.) fresh or dry active yeast

⅓ oz. (1 tsp.) extra virgin olive oil

In a mixing bowl, combine flours and salt. In a separate small mixing bowl, stir together 200 gr (about 1 cup) lukewarm water, yeast and olive oil, then pour it into the flour mixture. Knead w your hands until well combined, about 3 minutes, then let the mixture rest for 15 minutes.

Knead rested dough for another 3 minutes. Cut into 2 equal pieces and shape each into a round, seamless dough ball; it is important to have it round and smooth to make it easier t push the dough out and stretch the crust. Place the dough ball on a heavily-floured surface cover with a dampened cloth and let rest and rise for 3 to 4 hours at room temperature or for 8 - 24 hours in the refrigerator. (If you refrigerate the dough, remove it 30 - 45 minutes before you begin to shape it for pizza.)

To prepare the pizza crust, make sure the dough has come to room temperature. Begin to push the dough out from the middle to make the crust in your desired shape. Makes dough for 2 piz

NOTES

The Wayzata Bar & Grill is owned and operated by the City of Wayzata and has been a favorite gathering place for residents since 1947. Several moves and remodels have been made to keep the bar and restaurant and connected municipal liquor business contemporary. Affectionately known as "The Muni," the bar and restaurant is still a casual spot in town where locals can grab a drink, a bite to eat and listen to some music or catch a game.

The recent move across the street to a new location in 2011 provided a modern and bigger space while keeping the local charm that loyal patrons love. Friendly servers know your name and remember your usual order. With the benefit of having a liquor store under the same roof, the Wayzata Bar & Grill has a large selection to quench your thirst.

The expanded menu builds off of the favorites from the old location—burgers, "Muni Dogs," sandwiches and prime rib. The Wayzata Chilly Open Award Winning Chili and homemade soups are warm, tasty comforts for any day. A hearty bowl of their Creamy Artichoke Chicken Soup and a helping of the fresh and hot popcorn make a great meal at the place where "you are only a stranger once."

 # Wayzata Bar & Grill Creamy Artichoke Soup

INGREDIENTS

1 cup celery, diced

1 cup onion, diced

3 tbsp. butter

2 cups artichoke hearts, chopped

1 cup green chili peppers

1 tbsp. onion salt

1 tbsp. celery salt

1 tbsp. oregano

6 cups grilled chicken, diced

¼ cup lemon juice

¼ cup cider vinegar

12 oz. cream cheese

8 cups chicken broth

4 cups heavy cream

8 oz. frozen spinach

In a large pot cook celery and onions in butter until softened. Add artichoke hearts, green chilies, onion salt, celery salt, oregano, chicken, lemon juice, cider vinegar and cream cheese. Cook on low heat until cheese is softened and flavors combine.

Add chicken broth, cream and spinach and heat through. If desired, thicken with a mixture of equal parts butter and flour. Makes 2 ½ gallons.

NOTES

Wuollet Bakery has been a family-run business since the first bakery was established in 1944 by Reino Wuollet. Today, his grandsons run the business with the same grounded principles and passion for quality baked goods. Although the bakery business has evolved over the years, third generation owners Mike Jurmu, Jim Jurmu and Doug Wuollet take pride in the care and fine ingredients that go into every decadent item.

Wuollet Bakery Wayzata has been filling the breadbaskets and satisfying the sweet tooth of lake area residents since 1991. It is known for its specialty items—delicious tortes and pastries, beautifully crafted wedding cakes, unique European breads—but one of the everyday favorites are the famous Brownies Enormous. Thick, chewy and rich, they truly are enormously delicious.

 # Wuollet Bakery Brownie Enormous

INGREDIENTS

¾ cup butter, melted

4 squares unsweetened baking chocolate

2 cups sugar

3 large eggs

1 tsp. vanilla

1 cup flour

1 cup mixed large walnut pieces and chunks of premium-grade bar chocolate

Preheat oven to 350 degrees. In a glass mixing bowl, combine butter and baking chocolate and microwave on high until melted, about two minutes. Stir sugar into chocolate until well blended, add eggs and vanilla and stir again. Add flour and mix until blended. Gently fold in walnut and premium chocolate pieces being careful not to over-mix.

Pour into a 9 x 13" buttered baking dish and bake 30 – 35 minutes until toothpick in center comes out with fudgy crumbs. Cut into desired quantity of brownies. Serve as is or to make a more elaborate dessert, microwave brownie briefly and bury with a generous scoop of premium vanilla ice cream topped with fresh raspberries or another favorite seasonal fruit.

NOTES

In July 2012, locals John Klick, Patrick Foss and Jon Lewin started the Excelsior Brewing Company. Following an April 2014 expansion, they opened the doors to their current taproom that features 16 draught lines and a 3.5 barrel pilot system. It is employee-owned, many of whom grew up around the area.

Excelsior Brewing Company celebrates everything Lake Minnetonka has to offer. Located just a couple blocks from the lakefront, boaters can stop and sip a pint or get a growler to go. It's also a casual spot to meet friends, hear live music, take a tour and experience the many fun events.

Currently the brewery makes four flagship beers: XLCR American Pale Ale, Bridge Jumper IPA, Bitteschlappe Brown Ale and Big Island Blond, along with many seasonal offerings. So when you're making a recipe at home, be sure to pick up the Excelsior Brewing Company-paired brew to enjoy with it.

 # Excelsior Brewing Company Beer Pairings

Baked Ziti - *XLCR Pale Ale*
Beef Cheek Nachos - *Bitteschlappe Brown Ale*
Brownie Enormous - *Bitteschlappe Brown*
Campstyle Walleye - *Big Island Blond*
Cauliflower-Pancetta Soup - *Big Island Blond*
Cioppino - *XLCR American Pale Ale*
Creamy Chicken Artichoke Soup - *Big Island Blond*
Fresno pizza - *Bitteschlappe Brown Ale*
German Sauerkraut Soup - *XLCR Pale Ale*
Horseradish Crusted Salmon - *Bridge Jumper IPA*
Linzer Torte - *Bitteschlappe Brown*
Mediterranean Angel Hair Pasta - *XLCR Pale Ale*

Pub Burger - *XLCR Pale Ale*
Roasted Scottish Salmon Salad - *Bitteschlappe Brown*
Shady Island Chicken Sandwich - *Big Island Blond*
Skinny Chicken - *Big Island Blond*
Smoked Gouda/Lager Fondu - *Bitteschlappe Brown*
Smoked Lamb Shank - *XLCR Pale Ale*
Strawberry Watermelon Salad - *Bridge Jumper IPA*
Southwest Quinoa Salad - *Bridge Jumper IPA*
Tacos Al Pastor - *Big Island Blond*
Thai Chicken Salad - *Bridge Jumper IPA*
Wayzata Trojan Roll - *Bridge Jumper IPA*

Bitteschlappe Brown Ale 6.5% ABV, 25 IBU

Our traditional Munich-style brown ale features a medium body, with brisk carbonation and a malty sweetness that carries the beer to a soft finish.

- Medium-bodied, smooth, dark ale
- Flavors of caramel, toffee, and cocoa in the finish
- Robustly malted with lots of Vienna malt, lightly hopped with German hops
- Very easy drinking—brown is a color, not a flavor

Bridge Jumper IPA 7.5% ABV, 96 IBU

A malt-forward IPA dry hopped with a shipload of raw, whole hops. This IPA defines "extreme balance." An extreme malty sweetness on the front end with a huge hop bitterness to finish clean.

- Hints of Papaya, Passion fruit, lots of floral hops
- Dry hopped with whole leaf Chinook hops
- Nice hop bite with no sharp, lingering bitterness
- Smooth mouth feel

Big Island Blond 5.2% ABV, 33 IBU

A light-bodied, approachable ale with a perfect balance of malt and hops, accented by a subtle citrus flavor and aroma. The perfect every day beer. A patio pounder.
- Soft & biscuity
- Smooth without harsh bitterness
- Moderate citrus hop flavor
- Easy drinking, approachable

XLCR Pale Ale 5.8% ABV, 50 IBU

An amber-colored American pale ale that combines a moderate, pleasant floral hop aroma with a satisfying malt sweetness from specialty malts.
- Substantial malt presence
- Bready, biscuity, toasty
- Refreshing, with the malt balancing the hop bite
- Moderate mouth feel

ACKNOWLEDGEMENTS

What started out as a passion project turned out to be so much more; thank you to all the restaurants, bakeries and the brewing company that participated. Over the past year I so enjoyed getting to know the faces behind our favorite lake area spots, hearing their stories and their philosophies about the food they serve. Mostly, I appreciate their willingness to share a recipe—this book would not have been possible without their enthusiasm.

I also want to thank the Excelsior-Lake Minnetonka, Mound and Greater Wayzata Area Chambers of Commerce for all of the information about their respective cities, their farmers' markets, community events and photos. I learned more about our lake community ties to fresh food, the spirit behind each annual event and the excitement created by bringing us all together. A thank you to Gale Woods Farm as well for their information and photos.

This book has beautiful photographs due to amazing photographers who shared their art. A special thank you to Al Whitaker for all of the stunning Lake Minnetonka photos he generously shared—if you want one of these beauties yourself, contact him at ajwcaptures@gmail.com.

Mary Stacke is my loving next-door neighbor who edited this book with the highest level of detail. She is also part of my cheering squad and I owe her a huge thank you for her unwavering encouragement and support. Patrick Jarvis of Jarvis Design did a fabulous job designing the book to meet my extremely high standards—it was a pleasure working with a fellow foodie and lake-lover.

Thank you to Stephanie March—my favorite food writer whose witty blogs and articles for *Mpls. St. Paul Magazine* I read each week—for graciously writing the foreword to this book. A western suburb gal herself, I knew she'd set the tone perfectly.

Finally, thank you for buying *Lake Minnetonka Eats*! I hope this inspires you to try some new recipes, visit a restaurant that you haven't been to yet and keep supporting those you already love.

THANK YOU

RECIPE INDEX

- Baked Ziti 64
- Beef Cheek Nachos 28
- Beer Pairings 124
- Brownie Enormous 120
- Burb Sauce 108
- Campstyle Walleye 32
- Cauliflower-Pancetta Soup 68
- Cioppino 48
- Creamy Chicken Artichoke Soup ... 116
- Fresno Pizza 88
- German Sauerkraut Soup 96
- Horseradish-Crusted Salmon with Golden Beet Sauce 40
- Linzer Torte 92
- Mediterranean Angel Hair Pasta ... 56
- Pizza Dough 112
- Pub Burger 80
- Roasted Scottish Salmon Harvest Grain Salad 76
- Shady Island Chicken Sandwich ... 104
- Skinny Chicken 84
- Smoked Gouda & Lager Fondue 36
- Smoked Lamb Shank 60
- Strawberry Watermelon Salad 44
- Southwest Quinoa Salad 24
- Tacos Al Pastor 72
- Thai Chicken Salad 52
- Wayzata Trojan Roll 100